THE SIX FIGURE PODCAST

The Ultimate Guide To Turning Your Podcast Into A Sales Machine That Consistently Fill Up Your Sales Pipeline With High Paying Clients With No Audience, No List, And No Promotion

MAYOWA AJISAFE

THE BOOK COT

THE SIX FIGURE PODCAST

The Ultimate Guide To Turning Your Podcast Into A Sales Machine That Consistently Fill Up Your Sales Pipeline With High Paying Clients With No Audience, No List, And No Promotion

THE SIX FIGURE PODCAST: *The Ultimate Guide To Turning Your Podcast Into A Sales Machine That Consistently Fill Up Your Sales Pipeline With High Paying Clients With No Audience, No List, And No Promotion*

Published And Printed by The Book Cot

THE BOOK COT
www.TheBookCot.com
Hello@TheBookCot.com

FREE TRAINING

Discover the Exact System I Use To Land High-Ticket Clients with My Podcast, Made $7.2k in the First Two Weeks and $65k In 6 Months With >500 Downloads

The Step by Step process you can implement immediately to start getting 3 to 4 high-ticket clients every month from your podcast without increasing your podcast downloads, audience or subscribers.

Get instant access to the FREE Training at https://www.thesixfigurepodcast.com/training

TABLE OF CONTENTS

INTRODUCTION

If you picked up a copy of this book and reading this right now, I believe:

1. You have a podcast and like to use your podcast to sell your high-ticket service
2. You have a podcast and are looking for ways to make more money from your podcast.

Whichever group you belong to, this book will not only show you how to make more money from your podcast.

It will also show you a very smart and novel way to turn your podcast into a sales machine that fills in your sales pipeline with high-ticket clients using a podcasting sales system I called The High Ticket Podcast Sales System.

Everything you are about to learn in this book will change your mindset about the idea of podcasting as you have got to know. It will also open your mind up to the possibilities of using your podcast as a tool to bring in those high-paying clients for your high-ticket services, one you have never taught of or heard of before.

You are about to see a new world of possibilities of how powerful podcasting can be and how you have left so much money on the table by podcasting the way you know before.

But before anything...

WHAT BOOK IS ALL ABOUT

No doubt, podcasting has become a content marketing tool and a popular fad that almost everyone thinks they should jump on.

But wait a second.

This book isn't meant to tell you why you should start a podcast. If you are reading this book now, I feel you already have a podcast.

How do I know?

The title of this book is meant to only speak to people who have a podcast and need ways to make money from it or use their podcasts to bring in more clients for their businesses.

But if you are reading this and you don't have a podcast, then it's fine. What you will learn in this book will show you how not to start a podcast or do podcasting the way everyone is doing podcasting.

I bet you have read tons of posts about podcasting.
Lots of data must have been thrown to your face about how 40% of Americans now listen to podcasts or how many millions of blogs are out there.

At the same time, there are only tens of thousands of podcasts, and you can jump into the ship and the trend and make a killing for yourself with the Gary Vee style of jumping on the latest trend.

And this book won't teach you how to start a podcast.

Anyone, even my neighbor's dog, that annoyed me with his never-ending barking can start a podcast with just a mic and a free podcasting hosting platform like Anchor.

This book is written to teach you how to use podcasts unconventionally to make more money the way most podcasters won't think of and how you can turn your podcast into a sales machine that "prints" high-paying clients for your business consistently.

And ultimately, I will teach you how to use your podcast if you are a podcast newbie with no following, no email list, and even no credentials or clout online and get high ticket sales for your business.

And be warned, if you are the type that likes following the sayings and advice of your top internet celebrities and gurus or you are the type that likes to copy what everyone else is doing, then know this won't be a good idea for you.

This is because what you will learn in this book is the opposite of whatever advice you have heard from your podcasting guru or influencer.

But if you want to see podcasting from a different and unconventional angle for business growth and clients' accusations as a nobody in your field or space, then get a cup of your favorite drink and read this book to the last word of it.

WHO THIS BOOK IS FOR

Honestly, this book isn't for everyone.

This is a genuine claim and not just a bogus one.

If you are a service business owner who already has a podcast and runs, owns, or manages a business that sells a high-ticket offer and needs more clients for your business, this book might be for you.

And if you don't have a podcast but planning to start one and you have a service business that sells high ticket service, and you have been looking for a client accusation system that guarantees you predictable, measurable, consistent, and constant sales and marketing system that will sell your high ticket offer, then this book is for you.

If none of these applies to you, I am sorry, this book isn't for you.

If you have a podcast or planning to start one and you sell a low-ticket service or offer, this book won't help you much as it will help service business owners who sell high-ticket services.

CHAPTER 1:
THE PROBLEM WITH THE CONVENTIONAL PODCAST SYSTEM

I have had a lot of conversations with business owners either as a guest on The Six Figure Entrepreneur Podcast or as a prospective client who reached out to me.

Two common things I have noticed from those who have a podcast is that they believe a podcast is a good lead generation tool and a good way to make money.

I won't blame anyone for thinking this is true.

For years, I have always believed the same.

Because of this, I started three podcasts to get more leads for three different businesses in the past. I've also thought I could make money from selling my books and services, but those podcasts all failed, and I quit before I could publish my 20th episode.

If you look into how people consume podcasts, you will see that most people who do listen to podcasts or love listening to podcasts are not looking for something to buy but are looking for something they can learn.

This means a podcast isn't a sales tool, at least in the way you have been taught but an educational tool that can help nurture people looking for information to become a buyer over time.

And if you are to be objective, this sales system is a long process, and it takes time to turn those information seekers into paying clients.

This is the reason most podcasters quit and why most who don't quit don't make money from their podcasts.

The conventional podcast system is flawed.

It focuses on making money from the consumption side of podcasting.

This means you can only make money from people who listen to, download, or streams your podcast, and to make that happen, you must have a lot of people listening to your podcast.

For people who have a large following, email list, or big audience who listen to their podcast, this isn't much of a problem as someone like John Lee Dumas, who is one of the popular poster guys for making money with podcasting, has a large following in many forms. Thus the number is working well for him to make money from his podcast.

That is why people like Gary V, Tim Ferriss, Joe Rogan, and many other influencers who have a big following are making a killing with podcasting in one way or the other.

Thousands of people download, stream, and listen to their podcasts. So they can make money from channels like sponsorships and selling their book, products, or services.

But for someone who doesn't have such a large following, copying these influencers who have a large following makes most people who start a podcast with no significant audience size quit.

I was that guy for years.

That guy who starts a podcast hoping to use the podcast to build an audience and then sell to that audience down the line.

I've been that guy for years.

But at three different times, I failed in doing podcasting that way.

Take one thing away from this chapter.

Podcasting isn't a lead generation or a money-making tool if you don't have a large audience you can sell to.

This is why 90% of podcasters who don't have a large audience are making little or no money.

How do I know?

I have been one of them, and I have had a lot of conversations with podcasters who fit well into that picture.

But does that mean you can't make good money from your podcast or use your podcast to sell your high-ticket services if you are not John Lee Dumas or Lewis Howes?

Of course, you can't if you keep seeing making money and selling from the consumption side of podcasting.

But you can make a lot of money and even use your podcast to sell your high ticket services if you do the opposite of what every podcaster does by implementing the High Ticket Podcast Sales System you will learn in this book.

Mayowa Ajisafe

UP NEXT...

If you have read this chapter, you might be wondering who I am to tell you what your podcast guru or influencer has taught you about making money from podcasting is wrong.

But wait a second.

I didn't say what your podcasting guru has taught you is wrong.

What they have taught you works for them, and you already know why in this chapter.

It won't work for you if you don't have the audience size that drives those sales you've seen them talk about.

And I would like to tell you a story (my bad, I am a storyteller, I love stories and even host a podcast that gives six, seven, and eight-figure entrepreneurs a platform to tell their stories)

If what you have read in this chapter about the problem with what your podcasting guru has taught you isn't clear enough, the story in the next chapter will show you more about what I am talking about.

It will also show why you have not been able to make money from your podcast or use it to sell your high-ticket services.

CHAPTER 2:
MY PODCASTING JOURNEY AND WHAT YOU SHOULD LEARN FROM MY PAST PODCASTING FAILURE

MY PODCASTING JOURNEY

The year was 2013.

Some months earlier, I sacked my boss and left my dream job to pursue my dream of being an entrepreneur.

After the failure of my first business, a learning platform I called Learning Annex, the next idea that appeals to me apart from my newfound love for writing and book publishing is podcasting.

I started Your Career And You Podcast.

It was a solo podcast, and I used each episode to teach job seekers the same strategy I used to land my dream job in two weeks without any connections in an industry different from what I have the academic qualifications for.

I teamed up with the second biggest job-hunting website in my locality to syndicate my podcast to their website visitors and audience.

In two months, as crude as my podcast was (I was recording with my laptop's in-build mic), I built a list of 1600 subscribers and got an average of 1000 downloads for each podcast episode.

I have a platform and an audience to leverage, so I don't have traffic issues, but I wasn't making any money from the podcast.

I had some books I had written documenting all I was teaching, but nobody was buying them.

I was broke at this time and needed money, so I quit the podcast when I realized my target audience was broke people like me.

Two years later, in 2015, I got traction and some amazing results with my self-publishing blog - Authors Crib.

I was making money helping authors write, publish and market their books.

Then I started another podcast called the Authors Crib Podcast.

I interviewed self-publishing experts on the podcast to share their best tips for authors.

I made it to the then famed iTunes News and Noteworthy, beating podcasts created by many heavyweight online sensations like John Lee Dumas and Gary Vaynerchuck.

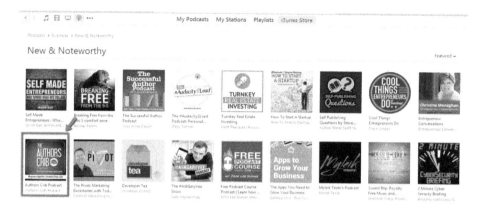

I don't have a money problem compared to where I was when I started my first podcast, but I had no plans for Authors Crib Podcast, and I didn't make it to my 20th episode before I quit.

My podcast failure continued in 2020 when I started another podcast with a friend, but we got so busy that the podcast went into the abyss of extinction after the 4th episode.

MISTAKES MOST PODCASTERS MAKE WITH PODCASTING AND WHEN STARTING A PODCAST

Most podcasts will never make it to the 30th episode, only a few will make it to the 50th, and even more, fewer will make it to the 100th episode.

This is because most people who start a podcast won't see any result in making money or selling their services or products, enough to give anyone cold feet about producing more episodes.

If you have a podcast or are planning to start one, here are the mistakes you should look for.

1. Having No Plan

One common theme with all my past podcasts is not having any plans for my podcasts.

This lack of planning starts with why I stated the podcasts and, in a realistic way, what I was trying then to achieve with the podcasts.

To say I don't have all these in mind before starting will be a lie.

The problem is that I only have a vague idea of what the podcasts are for and what I am trying to achieve with each one.

For example, I didn't have an audience in all those failed experiments, and I planned to use those podcasts to build an audience for myself.

Even when this worked for my first podcast, podcasting isn't the right tool to build an audience you can sell to if you don't have an audience before starting the podcast.

2. Starting A Podcast Without An Audience And Hoping To Use A Podcast To Build An Audience

Mistake number two is starting those podcasts to use them to build an audience.

Let's be real here.

Most podcasting gurus, books, and even courses out there will tell you podcasting is a good tool to build an audience from scratch, but this is a big lie that has pulled a lot of newbies who have no business starting a podcast to embrace the idea of starting one.

Most of these gurus had a large audience before they started their podcast, and I can mention names like Gary V, Tim Ferris, Pat Flynn, Lewis Howes, Joe Rogan, and the like.

For a guy like John Lee Dumas, who started the Entrepreneur On Fire Podcast without an audience, he has something else that worked for him when he started.

He might look like an exemption to what I just said, but deep down, he started a podcast that aired daily, something that had never been done before, and this gave him leverage called virility, and in no time, what he was doing became an internet sensation.

You can't also discount the fact that he knew a lot of top influencers who were guests on his podcast when he started, and because of how unique his podcast is, he was able to have those popular people with a large audience talk about him.

Don't make the mistake of thinking you will start a podcast as a newbie with just a handful of followers or none, an email list of 200 subscribers, no clout, and in 3 to 5 months, you would have built a large audience out of your podcast.

That was the lie I was telling myself then, and it got me with dashed hope after churning out episodes of my podcasts.

3. Starting A Podcast To Make Money From Selling Products Or Services To The Podcast Audience You Will Build From Podcasting

This is in line with what I said in mistake number two.

For guys with a big audience, it's easy to start a podcast and grow bigger while creating a way to make money from sponsors or selling products or services.

But for newbies who have no audience or have a small audience who planned to use podcasting to build a large audience, betting on making money from selling or sponsorships from a new podcast will be a dream that will take years.

And how many people can produce a weekly podcast for two straight years without making a dime but still be able to keep going?

Maybe none.

THE NEW WAY OF PODCASTING THAT GOT ME RESULTS

I've failed at Podcasting four times.

I've had big dreams for my podcasts, and they all melted away months after.

I never imagined going back to podcasting before I started The Six-Figure Entrepreneur Podcast.

15

But how did I arrive at going back to podcasting after my four earlier failures?

I've made money helping aspiring authors write and publish their dream books.

Business was good, and I only needed to wait for my client to reach out to me on a Fiverr platform.

That was what I have enjoyed for four years but in 2019, Fiverr changed their algorithm or something; my gigs and my profile were then sent to the pit of obscurity.

I used to make between $2500 and $6500 every month on Fiverr, but after this change, things started slowing down for months, and my income went down until early 2020 when clients stopped coming in from Fiverr.

That was when I realized I didn't own a client accusation system that had sent me clients for years.

While I had huge savings in the bank and an e-commerce store that was bringing extra cash, I knew I had to create my own clients' accusation system, one I could own and control.

Days turned into weeks and weeks into months and months into a year of buying courses, reading books, and consuming everything I could find about clients' accusation systems.

I kept asking myself what system I could build that would consistently bring clients that wouldn't involve running ads, building an email list, blogging, and webinars.

Almost all client accusation systems involve doing one or more of these things.

It took me a lot of money and wasted time to finally understand that all I was doing then won't give me what I wanted, which is a consistent, measurable, scalable system that I can completely control.

Talk of running paid ads; I have tried it.

I've spent thousands of dollars on Facebook ads for my e-commerce store, and I've made a lot of money from that, and I wish things are like that forever.

I've also used Facebook ads to sell many of my clients' books at Authors Crib to the point that I wrote and published two books about Facebook ads marketing for authors.

But unfortunately, I realized that Facebook ads work, but there is something called ad decay.

And ultimately, my ad account was banned.

That made the dream of consistent sales profitably from Facebook ads a one-hour night party that ended with everyone having to find their way home to their boring life.

As a guy who won't give up, I learned Google Display Ads and Youtube Ads after my Facebook Ads party ended.

That worked well also, and I made some good money from selling the same products I was selling using Facebook ads, but I ended up at the same spot I found myself with Facebook ads, except for the fact that I didn't have problems with my Google ads accounts been banned.

So you can see why I include using paid ads in the list of what I don't want to do even though I know that that clients' accusation system works.

It just doesn't guarantee long-term success, and I don't have control over what happens with my ads and ad accounts.

I have spent ample time on Pinterest to get more clients for my services and even hired someone to do that for me. It just doesn't work.

I have also tried blogging, but the traffic I got from running ads on my blog posts isn't just converting.

I have tried to use a tripwire offer to sell my publishing services. That one, too, only got me a couple of sales but did not convert to getting me paying clients.

I once tried cold emailing and invested in a $399 cold email course but after sending hundreds of cold emails, all I got was cricket.

Talk of posting on Instagram, I have tried it as well, but I quit after months of just adding more followers, and nobody is asking me about what I have to offer.

Before turning to podcasts, I have tried these to create a sales system that will solve my client accusation problems.

For years, I have wanted to start another podcast, but I don't want to start; I want to make sure I start one that will help my business and also help me build relationships with people who can become my client and referral partners, and JV partners.

DOING PODCASTING THE UNCONVENTIONAL WAY

After trying to do all I had learned about podcasting and failing three times at Podcasting, I knew things had to be different.

Damn the gurus; I knew I was not starting a podcast to build an audience.

I knew the odds were just against starting a podcast with my small audience and getting tons of downloads and listeners like I used to believe.

In the previous chapter, I mentioned the idea most podcasters always like to believe: making money from podcasting for them will come from the consumption side of podcasting.

I keep asking myself one question.

How do I turn this around to make podcasting work for me?

When you ask good questions, you will likely get good answers.

While I kept asking myself this question, an idea came to my mind.

What if I don't even create my podcast for listeners?

What if I only create my podcast for those I want to work with?

These questions opened up many possibilities for me, and after looking around, I keep seeing a few examples of people doing things differently with their podcasts.

One good example I saw who does podcasting differently is Max Traylor.

Then, a lightbulb went on in my head, and I decided to start The Six Figure Entrepreneur Podcast

Digging more to learn made me reach out to Max to be a guest on my then "soon-to-be-launched" podcast, and he said yes and became guest number six on The Six Figure Entrepreneur Podcast.

You can listen to my interview with Max Traylor at https://www.thesixfigureentrepreneur.com/max-traylor

When I started The Six Figure Entrepreneur Podcast, I knew my focus wasn't to use podcasting to build an audience but to use it to have conversations with my guests, who are also my ideal clients.

Now, this part is what I want you to pay attention to.

I just want to show you what I threw away in my thoughts, dreams, and beliefs when I started The Six-Figure Entrepreneur Podcast.

These are things most podcast gurus will tell you to focus on or believe when starting a podcast, but I just knew following those things or focusing on them won't land me anyway near my aim for starting the podcast.

It might be hard for you to understand why I don't care about these things, but along the line, in this book, you will understand.

1. I Don't Need To Build An Audience, Get Tons Of Downloads, Or Land A Big A-List Guest Like Gary Vee And Other Stuff New And Old Podcasters Aim For.

I sell high ticket services, and I only need to make one or two sales a month to reach my revenue goal for my business.

You will understand what I am talking about if you have a service-based business that sells high-ticket services.

So I know I don't need to build a big audience to make money from podcasting.

The only audience that matter are people whom I like to have conversations with, and I want to give them as much value as I can during and after my time having a conversation with them.

While the conventional podcast system I have used teaches me that I should be creating content FOR my audience.

Now, I am creating content WITH my target audience, mostly busy six, seven, and eight-figure entrepreneurs who might need my help.

And with my podcast format, I am achieving the two goals at the same time.

2. My Main Goal Is To Create Content With Just One Set Of People - My Guest. Anyone That Consumes My Content As A Listener Is A Bonus For Me.

I don't need to build a big audience, and I only want to build an audience of people who might need my help.

With this in mind, metrics like the number of downloads I have is something I won't care about.

I don't want to have any sponsors for my podcast. The only sponsor I need is my business.

Let me real here

People who make good money from sponsorships have thousands and tens of thousands of downloads per episode, which attract sponsors to want to pay them to reach their listeners.

To get to that level where you can get those numbers of downloads, you need to have a large audience, and as a newbie who doesn't have such an audience size, it will take years of hard work and showing up to reach that level.

Why would I bet anything on reaching that level to make a dime from my time creating my podcast content?

In less than three weeks of starting my podcast this way, I have landed a $7500 deal and made $20k in the first two months with no reviews and less than 1000 downloads.

I don't care about how many downloads I am getting, but I know those downloads will come big at a point down the road, and those will be a bonus that I can then leverage for more opportunities.

Numbers like who is subscribing to Apple Podcast or the number of reviews I get don't matter to me either.

I don't need those things now and maybe in the nearest future.

3. My Guests Are The Hero Of My Show. The Show Isn't About Me As An Expert In Anything Or Even About My Stories But About Theirs.

Two of my past Podcasts are about me and my stories.

The other one is about my area of expertise which is book publishing.

This time, I didn't start a podcast about me, what I know, what I do, or even my stories as an entrepreneur.

The Six Figure Entrepreneur Podcast is all about my guest; they are the hero and everything that matters.

Let me show you something interesting here.

Have you ever seen Oprah Winfrey talking about herself on her show?

She doesn't do that.

She is busy shining the spotlight on amazing people across the globe, and her platform is for them to share their stories.

She is a media guru and one of the few media gurus I want to emulate or follow.

I only want to build an audience of those who might need my help, and these are busy entrepreneurs with a book to write.

If I started a podcast about book publishing, do you think all the busy and successful entrepreneurs I have interviewed on my podcast will ever say yes to me?

Of course not.

This is because they don't care about book publishing, even if they want to write a book, but they care about telling their stories.

That's why I've only got two NOs from all my email outreach to have these amazing people as a guest on my podcast.

If I started a podcast about book publishing, I would need to build an audience of people who want to write a book, so I can sell my high-ticket services to them, which will take me years to achieve.

But why wait for years when I can walk another path to get the same results in weeks?

Yes, I made $7500 within three weeks of starting The Six Figure Entrepreneur Podcast.

I did that without spending a dime on ads, without blogging, without posting anything on social media, and without an audience.

In short, just like Oprah Winfrey's show, her guests are the hero, and she makes them one - no wonder people's fortune changes after they appear on her show.

I am not Oprah, and I don't dream of becoming one, but in my little space, I want to make everyone who appears as a guest on my podcast to be the hero.

And to do this, I try to make my time with them lovely and give them bits of content they can share with friends, family, and their audience.

For every published interview, my team creates audiograms of valuable lessons, insights, or stories they share during the interview and sends them to them.

They can use them in whatever way they want, and I plan to add more to that to make their time with me worthwhile.

UP NEXT...

In this chapter, you have got to learn what led to me turning podcasting off of what it used to be with my three past podcasts.

This book is written, and all you will learn in it will only work for businesses that sell high ticket services in one form or the other.

And by high ticket services, I mean services priced from $2000 and above.

The reason for this is very simple.

The High Ticket Podcast Sales System works don't favor businesses with low ticket service to sell.

The system is driven mostly by conversations with your ideal clients on your podcast.

If you have a low-priced service or products like a book, a $599 course, or a $299 membership plan, the time and resources you will need to implement The High Ticket Podcast Sales System won't be worth the result you get from your podcast in terms of sales.

I spend between $1500 and $2000 monthly to produce my podcast, and I can keep doing that because I have a high ticket service that brings in more than that for me every month from my podcast.

You can now see why this won't work for me if I have to spend that much and make $599 Or $999 in sales from a low ticket service or offer.

In the next chapter, I will show you why podcasting is a great solution for your high-ticket service business to fix your client accusation problem.

CHAPTER 3:
WHY A SIX FIGURE PODCAST IS THE SOLUTION TO FIX YOUR HIGH TICKET SALES PROBLEM

Let's be real here.

Relationships and conversation are the basis of your business as a high-ticket service business owner.

When you sell a $10k done for your service as I do, you won't expect anyone to pay you such an amount by clicking on your ads and buying a $39 tripwire offer before handing over their $10k to buy your high ticket offer.

This might work once for a few people who are in the ready-to-buy phase of the sales system.

Still, it's not sustainable or scalable, and neither would it bring you the consistent result that you can measure and duplicate simultaneously, and ultimately, you don't control much.

Your ads can stop working at any time while your ads account isn't in your control, and you don't even have control over who sees your ads and when they see them.

Or can anyone pay $10k by just sending a cold email to them offering your service?

Your ideal clients for your high ticket service don't buy because of your ads, because you post on social media, and neither they buy from you because you post content on your blog or read your post on someone else blog.

They buy from you because they have a problem; they know you have a solution to their problem and have some form of trust in you or your business that you can solve it.

The issue with most sales systems you have been used to is that they don't help much or in any way to build a relationship with your ideal clients and create that trust factor as soon as possible to make your ideal clients see you as a solution to their problem.

This relationship and trust problem is what the High Ticket Podcast Sales System solves.

I hate treating my ideal clients or prospective clients as robots. I can just send to a sales page with sweet work, pass them through some email sequence to "nurture" them, and make them from me.

They are humans.

They crave relationships, conversation with other humans, and a connection with other humans.

So why treat them like they aren't human with sales systems email sequence, a long sales page, or a two-hour webinar full of you pitching what you sell?

This question drove my resolve only to explore a sales system that can help me have a relationship and connection with my ideal clients from a real human-to-human conversational point of view.

The Six Figure Entrepreneur Podcast has helped me enjoy a stellar medium where I can have conversations with my ideal clients, referrals partners, and even people I can collaborate with to get more clients for my business.

Almost every day, I have my calendar filled up with scheduled calls with my ideal clients and people I can collaborate with to get more business.

And it also gives me a platform where I can invite anyone I want to do business with or do business with to a conversational table to get to know each other and relate. If we are a good fit, we can talk about business and how we can work together.

It also gives me a platform where the "Sales" part of selling a high ticket service can be removed, and we all can enjoy a good time relaxed friend-to-friend environment.

Here is why starting a podcast or rebranding your existing one using The High Ticket Podcast Sales System is the solution to fixing your high ticket sales problem while filling up your sales pipeline with a consistent supply of ideal clients in a way you can measure, scale up and control.

1. CONVERSATIONS ARE THE BASIS ON WHICH PEOPLE BUY HIGH TICKET SERVICES.

You run ads, do a webinar, and set up a trip wire funnel to have calls with many of your prospective clients.

The High Ticket Podcast Sales System gives you a medium to have a lot of these conversations with your ideal clients in a "non-sales-y" way, and your ideal clients will love the idea of having those conversations with you because they are coming into that conversations without the pressure of them knowing you are selling to them.

2. WITH ADS AND ALL THOSE OTHER SALES SYSTEMS, YOU ARE NOT IN CONTROL OF WHO COMES YOUR WAY.

Using The High Ticket Podcast Sales System, you have absolute control over whom you talk to, who walks into your sales pipeline, and who doesn't.

I love this because it gives me so much power to choose whom I want to talk to or work with rather than all other systems that put the control in the hands of your prospective clients and a third-party platform that you don't control or own.

3. HAVING A SIX FIGURE PODCAST USING THE HIGH TICKET PODCAST SALES SYSTEM REMOVES THE NEED FOR YOU TO SELL THE WAY YOU HAVE TO USING ALL THE OTHER SALES SYSTEMS YOU MIGHT HAVE TRIED BEFORE.

When you invite your ideal clients to have conversations with you using The High Ticket Podcast Sales System, you don't need to sell to them.

You have conversations to get to know them, what they want, what they are looking for, and if both parties like each enough to work together and if you know you can help them, working together is easy.

This is good news for you if, like me, you are not a natural salesman and you don't like the idea of selling to anyone or pressuring anyone to buy from you.

4. A SIX-FIGURE PODCAST USING THE HIGH TICKET PODCAST SALES SYSTEM ALLOWS YOU TO MAKE YOUR PROSPECTIVE CLIENTS FEEL GOOD AND SPECIAL ABOUT THEMSELVES.

This system is where everything isn't about you but your ideal clients.

I love that I don't need to talk about myself but spend all my time letting my prospective clients talk about themselves, feel good about themselves and what they do, and have the spotlight shining bright on them.

I have shared my stories and talked about my journey in this book. That is because it's a book, and as readers, you aren't listening to me speak as I do on my podcast.

My stories shared here are part of what I need to do for you to get to know me and why I am writing this book and why you should care about all I said in this book.

But for my podcast, I have a more personal connection with them, and they aren't on my podcast to hear about me or have me share my stories with them.

Instead, they talk about themselves and what they do; that is one thing I offer them as a guest.

This system gives them so much that they will like and trust you in a short time enough to make them want to buy from you if you are both a good fit for each other.

5. THE HIGH TICKET PODCAST SALES SYSTEM HELPS YOU SHORTEN THE SALES CYCLE AND COMBINES SALES AND MARKETING INTO ONE.

Most of your sales will come from trust, relationships, and conversation as a high-ticket service business owner.

These are three things that The High Ticket Podcast Sales System provides for you, and based on how the system work, your ideal clients get to like who you are and see you as someone they want to work with more easily than if you are trying to get them using all other systems.

When you have friendly conversations with them to get to know them and know much about what they do, it condenses sales and marketing into one and shortens the sales cycle if you implement the system correctly.

I can go on and on about why The High Ticket Podcast Sales System is a stellar solution to your high ticket sales problem and why you won't have to go through the famine and feast seasons you might have been experiencing in your business.

But like they say, the pudding taste is in the eating. The next chapters of this book will show why The High Ticket Podcast Sales System is the ultimate thing that will 10x your sales revenue.

6. EVEN WITH THE WORLD'S BEST SALES AND MARKETING SYSTEM, EVERYONE YOU HAVE A CONVERSATION WITH ABOUT WHAT YOU DO WILL BECOME PAYING CLIENTS. THE HIGH TICKET PODCAST SALES SYSTEM OFFERS YOU A GREAT FOLLOW-UP SYSTEM

The High Ticket Podcast Sales System has the perfect system to follow up with your ideal clients who aren't in the "ready to buy now" phase.

I have always struggled with how I will follow up with people I have had conversations with as prospective clients in the past.
I just don't like being that guy who keeps disturbing people in the guise of following up.

But The High Ticket Podcast Sales System has helped me solve everything.

With this system, you don't need to disturb anyone, and you also don't need to feel like you are doing too much to follow up with them.

UP NEXT...

In this chapter, I have shown you why a Six Figure Podcast using The High Ticket Podcast Sales System is a better solution to your high ticket client accusation problem.

But if you are like me (I am a curious cat), you would have been asking yourself what the High Ticket Podcast Sales System is and how you can create a Six-Figure Podcast using the system.

In the next chapter, you will learn what The High Ticket Podcast Sales System is and how to use the system to fill up your sales pipeline with high-paying clients consistently and in a scalable manner.

You will be blown away by what you learn in the next chapter.

CHAPTER 4:
FILL UP YOUR SALES PIPELINE WITH HIGH PAYING CLIENTS WITH A SIX FIGURE PODCAST

WHAT THE HECK IS HIGH TICKET PODCAST SALES SYSTEM

There are many ways to sell high ticket offers, and you should have known all of them or even tried one or more of these ways in the past.

But the problem with most of these ways is that they are relationship-based, even if ways like email list building, webinars, and posting on social media are sold as a relationship-based client accusation system.

Many set up funnels to attract, nurture, and turn cold leads into paying clients. Still, the flaw with this system is that it never mimics or recreates an environment that facilitates the idea of human-to-human conversations.

When you use a webinar to try to sell a high ticket offer, we all know you are not building any relationship with the leads the webinar brought your way.

With webinars, you are only selling and pitching to them under the guise of providing value.

So, your webinar is just a disguised way to take between forty minutes and two hours of your people's time with a sales pitch.

Such a system gives you so much leverage most time and gives little or nothing back to your ideal clients

Even if you give them some value during the webinar, you still need to hold something back from them enough to make them want to buy the high-ticket offer that you pitch at the end of the webinar.

What about posting on social media or posting in groups?

We all know you are not building any meaningful relationship doing that but are only interested in selling your high ticket offer o anyone who seems to need what you have to offer.

Strategies like tripwire funnels also aren't giving you any meaningful connection with your ideal audience. You are just selling to them by taking them through your tripwire funnel and nothing more.

The email list is the worst culprit here.

People are not robots; you can just run ads to a landing page, offering them a lead magnet and selling them with a series of emails you have automated to be sent out in drips.

I can go on and on with the flaws of all the client accusation systems you have been using or know about.

But I won't stop at that.

If you are selling a high-end, high-ticket product or service to the kind of people who buys such, do you think they are on Facebook scrolling through your ads, knowing, liking you, and trusting you enough to buy your $5,000 or $10,000 service or product?

Of course, your ideal client doesn't have the time to be browsing Facebook all day or watch endless videos on Youtube to make them see your ads to buy from you.

And if they see your ads, do you think they will send $5000 or more to a stranger they never know anything about?

Of course, you won't do that, and they won't do that as well.

Now, enough of all these.

People buy from people they like, know and trust.

That's for sure.

And as humans, the basis of any relationship whatsoever is conversations.

I had conversations with my wife when we met on a high-profile matchmaking platform, and today, we are happily married.

You never had friends with whom you didn't have one form of conversation before you became friends.

Do you?

Of course not.

Conversations fuel all human relationships, and any sales or marketing strategy that doesn't play to that idea or facilitate it is bound to fail you in your pursuit of landing sales for your high ticket offers.

At this point, you might tell yourself that we all know the best way to land a high-paying client is to get them on sales calls.

Yes, that is true; at least, that has been the only way I have been doing business since 2013, when I started my publishing company - Authors Crib.

But what if you have a system that fills your calendar with calls that leads to conversations that aren't sales calls or look like one?

While those conversations happen in an environment where your ideal clients win, and you also win, a relationship that might lead to a sale, friendship, referrals, or even a pure human-to-human relationship over time.

The best part is that you are not chasing anyone to have those conversations with you; you don't need to run ads to reach your target audience ad have them book a call with you.

You don't need to build any funnel, post on social media, blog, or do anything like anything many do to get clients online.

And to cap it all, you are creating tons of useful content with your ideal clients, not for them.

While you don't need to create any content by yourself, your ideal clients do the content creation with you and for you!

The High Ticket Podcast Sales System is the only client accusation system that I know does all of these for you while filling your sales pipeline up with conversations with your ideal client that leads to sales and many other benefits.

OVERVIEW OF THE HIGH TICKET PODCAST SALES SYSTEM

The basis of The High Ticket Podcast Sales System is having conversations that aren't sales calls with your ideal clients, with that conversation happening in an environment that allows you to get to know your ideal client.

They also have the chance to get to know you enough to want to do business with you if you are a perfect fit for each other, while they are also creating content with you that you can turn into different forms of content for your other ideal clients and your core audience.

Yes, such a system exists, and you are about to get to know what powers it and how to set up that system for yourself and your business.

There are many ways to set up this system, but none has the potency that podcasting has.

Wait a minute!

You might be wondering if this book is all about selling podcasting to you.

No, it's not.

This system is not about podcasting, but it is powered by podcasting.

Let me show you how the system works.

HOW THE HIGH TICKET PODCAST SALES SYSTEM WORKS

Since the best way to sell a high ticket offer is to get on a call with your ideal client, you want to have a way to invite your ideal client to have a friendly conversation with you that doesn't resemble or is a sales call while you both can decide if you are a good fit to work together.

This is where podcasting comes in.

You can't contact your ideal client to have a conversation with you if you don't give them enough reason to say yes to you.

Will you reply to any email asking you to get on a call with them to have a conversation for no reason?

Of course, you won't, and your ideal clients won't do the same either.

But if you have a podcast that speaks to your ideal clients, it can give them a good reason and a platform to talk about themselves and share their stories, expertise, and much about what they do.

Do you think your ideal clients will say no to you contacting them to be a guest on your podcast to talk about themselves while you have the time to get to know them well?

They get to know what you do, and you can have a conversation that leads to them becoming your client if you both see each other as a good fit to work together.

Of course, they will say yes most of the time.

That is how podcasting can help you implement The Conversation-Based High Ticket Sales System.

Although you can implement this system using other channels like creating a blog post with them, writing a book with them, and doing surveys with them, podcasting is the best way I have seen that shortens the timeframe of using this system.

The system works like this.

Step 1 : Your Dream Clients

The first step is to list whom you want to interview.

The three categories of people you want to interview on your Podcast are:

1. Your ideal clients.
2. Potential referral partners.
3. Influencers in your space who have the audience you can talk to.

Depending on your pressing sales need, whom you focus more on in these three categories of people will depend on what your immediate goal is.

I focused on interviewing people who fit well into the picture of whom I want my ideal clients to be. Although that picture changed twice in 3 months, I didn't bother to look for referrals or people I could collaborate with.

You can focus on one of these categories and mix things by focusing on two or more categories of people from that list if you can afford to do so.

Mind you; you don't need a list of 1000 people.

The beauty of using The High Ticket Podcast Sales System is that, unlike most other sales systems, you don't need to reach many people. It's so focused and precise that you only need from 20 to 30 people on your list for a start to get go.

You can add to this list later as you need to do so.

Step 2 : Start A Six Figure Podcast

Step two is to start your Six Figure podcast.

This is one important part of the process, and you need to pay attention to it.

In step 1, you have made a list of your ideal client, referral partners, or influencers you can collaborate with.

This step is where you start a podcast that speaks well and adds value to your target guests.

Your podcast should not be about you, what you do, or your business. It should be about a topic your ideal guests will like and be interested in.

For example, my target guests on The Six Figure Entrepreneur Podcast are entrepreneurs who have built a six or seven-figure business.

My podcast format is an interview-style one where I spotlight my guests, asking them questions that will help them share their entrepreneurial journey, what they do, lessons they have learned along their journey, and so much more.

My business publishes business books and produces a podcast for these six, and seven-figure entrepreneurs.

My podcast isn't named "The Business Book Podcast" or "The Six-Figure Podcast Show."

Let's say I have named my podcast any of the two names above.

In that case, it won't be of any interest to my target guests, and this is because even though they need a business book and a six-figure podcast, they don't care about talking about writing a business book or podcasting.

But with a podcast like The Six Figure Entrepreneur Podcast, they are interested in talking about their entrepreneurial journey and a lot about them and their businesses.

The interview-style podcast is the best podcast format that works well for The Hight Ticker Podcast Sales System.

A solo-style podcast or an educational-style podcast won't work.

Although there are ways, you can use a solo style podcast or an educational podcast to get clients, these styles of podcasts don't fit well into what you are trying to achieve with The High Ticket Podcast Sales System.

These styles of podcasts work best as a tool to nurture people who have found you online, contacted you, or sitting on the fence about working with you till they become paying clients.

The details of how to do that are beyond what I teach in this book.

Step 3 is reaching out to your target guest.

Do you just pick up your phone and call your target guest?

Do you use email?

What does the outreach look like when you are reaching out to someone who fits well into the picture of your ideal target guest and a potential target for the service(s) you provide?

After doing a lot of guest outreach myself, I can tell you the answer is simple.

You can use Linkedin, the good old email, and even reach out to your ideal guest with a DM on Twitter, Instagram, or Facebook.

My favorite outreach system remains email, which is just a personal preference as I am intentionally not active on most social media platforms, including Linkedin.

If you need something to get you started, go with email or Linkedin for a start.

Either via email or Linkedin, you want to make sure you follow up after your initial outreach if you didn't hear any reply from your first outreach.

I have seen followups emails account for more than half of the responses and guest bookings I had for my podcast. Some won't just notice the initial email, or maybe it escaped into the spam/junk folder.

You want to make sure you have at least two follow-up emails that you can send like four days after your initial outreach, and for those who won't reply after 3 or 4 follow-ups, you just need to move on and forget about them.

To make your guest booking process easier, you want to use a scheduling tool to help your guest book a time on your Calender to have the interview with you.

For a start, you don't need much bell and whistle for scheduling; Calendly will work just fine.

After your outreach, the next step is:

Step 4 : Interview Your Guest

Which is the actual interview.

Eventually, from your outreach, you will be getting responses and many saying yes to your request, and they will schedule a time to have the interview with you.

This is where you give them the opportunity to talk about themselves, what they do, and every other information you want to know about them.

This is your show, remember? You can ask them any question you want as long as it's a question that gets them to talk about themselves and their business.

I only talk for a tiny fraction of the period of my interview with my guests. I allow them to talk more, where I get to know them a lot to see how best I can help them.

Prepare your questions before you hit the record button. Make sure you ask them questions that will help them be the hero of the show and ones that will also allow you to get to know them much better.

I love to ask my guest one question, and that question helps me to know if they are people I can help. For those that respond in a way that shows me I can help them, I simply ask them if they need help with their book project and if they say yes, I just invite them to have another call with me to discuss ways I can help them birth their book to life.

Most of my guests are my ideal clients and need what I have to offer, but only a few are ready to have that problem solved by someone, and those are the ones that turn into paying clients faster.

For the rest who needs your help but, for one reason or the other, don't need help immediately; you can follow them up over time.

When it is time for them to solve the problem you solve with your service, you will stay on top of their mind, and even along the way, if you do a good job of following up, they can send referrals your way.

Another way to take your conversation to the next level without being a salesman many people hate.

You can ask them where they are going and what they want to achieve in the next few years.

And the thing is this - they will answer every single time because they have plans they are excited about and want to share with people.

Their answers will give you insights into their goals and aspirations, and you will begin to see where you can be of help and a source of value for them.

For your interview, show up with an open mind and a mind to have fun and a friendly conversation with your guests.

I have seen sales conversations popping up without bringing them up myself after I had an amazing time interviewing some of my guests.

People do business with and buy from people they like and trust. Your time with them on your interview call is a good time to build that like and trust that can open doors of opportunities for you.

Your focus should be more on the relationship you can build with your guests over time.

The money and the sales are just a bonus if you implement The High Ticket Podcast Sales System, and I am living proof of that.

The next step is Step 5

Step 5 : Produce The Interviews

This step is where your interview is edited, produced, and published.

You shouldn't bother yourself much with handling anything in this step.

The best option is to get someone to handle all you need to do in this step.

I wasted a lot of time and energy doing all the editing and production of my podcast interview for the first ten podcast episodes, but I was almost burned out from doing all of that even though I had the technical know-how to do them.

Outsource this part and show up to interview your guests and serve them.

Visit www.thesixfigureentrepreneur.com/podcast-production-call to book a call with me to get help with editing, producing, and publishing your podcast episodes. I will hook you up with a production team that can help you handle all of these.

I so much love the 80/20 Pareto principle.

Almost all of your sales success will come from whom you are interviewing and the interview you are having with them, and these two are what you should focus your time and energy on.

The rest are just 80% that will bring you 20% of the result, and these are things you should outsource.

Step 6 : Follow-up And Closing

Step 6 is the follow-up and ultimtely closing the sale.

You can ignore this step but know you will be leaving a lot on the table by not having a good follow-up system to put you in the mind of your podcast guest over time and help you build a relationship with them.

There are a lot of ways you can follow up with your podcast guests.

One of the ones I have seen that works well is what you will learn later in this book.

These six steps, if well-implemented, look simple and kind of basic, but they change the trajectory of your business result for good.

Now that you have the gist of setting up The High Ticket Podcast Sales System, I will take things to another level for you in the next chapter.

In the next chapter, I will show you how to use The High Ticket Podcast Sales System to turn on a floodgate of referrals for your business without feeling sales-y.

UP NEXT...

This book doesn't have the space for me to show you how you can use The High Ticket Podcast Sales System to 10x your business revenue.

I don't want this book to end up being a 300-page textbook that you can't read at a go.

I have used The High Ticket Podcast Sales System to create an on-demand referral system for my businesses, and it's the same system that has helped me fix my follow-up problems.

I have detailed all of this in one of my books - **The High Ticket Sales System:** *The Ultimate Guide To Consistently Filling Up Your Sales Pipeline With High Paying Clients With A Podcast*

You should get a copy of that book.

One of the amazing things about The High Ticket Podcast Sales System is that I have since discovered how I can combine the many useful ways a podcast can help my business with all the advantages and benefits of having a published book.

This kind of marriage I have discovered between a six-figure podcast and a six-figure business book turns out to be a very powerful combo that has the power to take your business to the level you never dreamed of in a short period.

This book you are reading is an example of what I love to call a Six Figure Business Book, just as my other book - **The High Ticket Podcast Sales System**, is one.

I wrote these two books for a reason.

While my podcast is a machine that fills up my sales pipeline with high-ticket clients on demand, these books are to be my passive selling machine, and making them work together created a massive effect on the results I am getting.

In the next chapter, I will show you how you can combine your Six Figure Podcast and a Six Figure Business Book to 10x the result you can get from The High Ticket Podcast Sales System.

In the next chapter, your mind is about to be blown away by what you will discover in it.

Now, let me let out the whole gist.

CHAPTER 5:
A SIX FIGURE BUSINESS BOOK AND A SIX FIGURE PODCAST: A POTENT HIGH TICKET SALES SYSTEM COMBO

I've written quite some business books as a tool to show my expertise and generate inbound leads, and I have helped business owners do the same.

For my first business book, a book about Facebook Ads Marketing For Authors, I made more than $30k off of leads that contacted me after reading the book to help them market their books using Facebook ads.

That book took me two days to write and only cost $2.99.

The amazing thing about that book is that I don't make much from selling the book. Most of what I made from the book came from authors reading it, getting in touch with me to ask me to help them sell their books using Facebook ads.

But until I launched The Six Figure Entrepreneur Podcast, I never understood what a business, lead generation style book can do when it's been used with a podcast.

So far in this book, I have shown you the power of implementing The High Ticket Podcast Sales System to get more high-paying clients.

But in this chapter, I am talking about things further for you.

I will show you how a book and your podcast can turn around the fortune of your business for good in The High Ticket Podcast Sales System ecosystem.

For all you have learned in this book so far, you are using your podcast to create a powerful outbound sales machine that will fill up your sales pipeline with high-quality ticket-paying clients, but in this chapter, you will learn how a book in The High Ticket Podcast Sales System can add more spices to your inbound sales machine to your sales pipeline.

WHY THE NEED FOR A SIX FIGURE BUSINESS BOOK?

1. When People Read Books, They Do So Because They Want To Solve A Problem Or Learn More About How To Solve A Problem

If you have the right Six Figure Business Book like I always love to help my client with, you are talking to your ideal clients about what you know and how you can help them solve the problems they have, and why you are the best person, they should hire to help them solve their problem.

A Six Figure Business Book is a good opportunity to attract your ideal clients to you to help them know about what you know and how you can help them.

I call a Six Figure Business Book the 24/7/365 sales machine that will help you do the selling even when you are sleeping.

Your ideal prospects know about your book by positioning it where they can easily see it.

It caught their attention, and they get a copy, read it, and with this, you have done a good job of showing them who you are (in a subtle way anyway), what you know and how you can help.

And if you write your book, The Six Figure Business Book way, you are giving them the next step they should take, which is reaching out to you in any way you want to work with you

With this, you don't need to sell them again; they already know what you know and how you can help them.

The sales process has been made easy for you, and all you need to do is talk to them and take the relationship to the next level.

2. As An Author, You Become An Instant Expert And An Authority In Your Industry

No tool gives you instant authority and expert status like a Six Figure Business Book.

A real estate company once contacted me a few weeks after publishing my first business book to help market their new lead generation book.

I wasn't surprised because I have shown readers in my book how Facebook ads can be used for book marketing.

That contact made me $3600 then.

Some years ago, Ed, a dating coach, reached out to me after reading one of my books about self-publishing.

That was when I hadn't figured out how to write a well-positioned business book.

I ended up helping him to write a book that teaches men how to stop being nice guys.

That book helped Ed launch his dating coaching business and brought him many paying clients.

In 2015, I once bought a book written by a dating coach; that book helped me to up my game with the woman I was meeting then. I hired a dating coach to help me with my dating game.

That, to me, was a no-brainer sale. I had read his book to understand he knew a lot about what I was trying to solve, and when I needed more personalized help, I reached out to him and paid him to coach me.

From that book, I am sure he would have made a lot from guys like me who read the book and later hired him.

That's the power of a Six Figure Business Book.

When you write a Six Figure Business Book, your ideal prospects will perceive you as an expert and authority on the topic you write about, which assures them that you know enough to help them solve their problems.

3. A Six Figure Business Book Is Valuable and Have A High Level Of Worth

Lead magnets are good, and they work for those who use them.

When you sell a high ticket service for high-worth people with little or no time to be looking for freebies and lead magnets to consume, you want to take your lead generation game to a higher level.

Books are valuable, and because of the time, energy, money, and efforts that go into writing and publishing a book, people see books as something that has a higher value than a few-page pdf, a cheat sheet, or some other types of lead magnets.

Even when people don't read your book immediately, they have it and will always see it and separate you from everyone offering other forms of lead magnets.

If you have identified and made a list of your dream clients, sending them a book in the mail with a short note and your contact details will surely do a better job than asking them to subscribe to be on your email list with the promise of a pdf or a cheat sheet.

4. Six Figure Business Books Are Scalable

With a Six Figure Business Book, you write and publish it once, delivering results for you 24 hours a day, seven days a week, and 365 days a year without much effort.

It also offers a tool to help you reach more people at scale without extra effort.

I can talk about what a Six Figure Business Book can do for your business and why you should have one for a whole day if I have the chance.

These four points are enough to make you understand what a Six Figure Business Book can do for you and your business to 10x your revenue and get more leads for your service business.

HOW TO WRITE A SIX FIGURE BUSINESS BOOK THE EASY WAY

For almost everyone I have interviewed on The Six Figure Entrepreneur Podcast, I have asked about what book they will like to write, and they all said they wanted to write a book and give me the picture of the book they wanted to write.

But most of these amazing entrepreneurs don't have the time or know-how to write a book.

And if you are reading this, you might wonder how you can write a book when you are not a writer, don't have the time, or even think writing a book is one big deal that you need thousands of green dollars and years to write.

If you have had these thoughts, I will say writing a Six Figure Business Book should and isn't any of that difficult.

There is a way to skip the writing and not do everything that does writing and publishing a book difficult.

When my team and I at The Book Cot work with our clients, we have our clients tell us about their book idea at www.thebookcot.com/consult.

We work with them to drill down to the basics of what they want their book to be and whom they are targeting.

We then help them create an outline that will deliver on the goal we have for our Six Figure Business Books.

Our goal is simple.

We want each Six Figure Business Book to serve as a tool that showcases our clients as an expert and authority and the best solution provider for their ideal clients and also a tool to make their ideal clients who will read the book reach out to them to get their problem solved.

We then take the outline and interview our clients to talk about what we have on the outline one after the other.

We then transcribe those recorded files into written words.

Our editors will now work on the transcribed words and turn them into a book manuscript.

We then do all the book production and publish the book.

Within two and three months, you can have a compelling Six Figure Business Book this way, and you won't write a single word.

Note the purpose of a Six Figure Business Book isn't to make money from book royalty or to become a USA Today or Wall Street Journal best seller.

You don't need all of that.

Your Six Figure Business Book is just an inbound sales machine to make the job of selling easy for you all around the clock.

Your Six Figure Business Book As a Tool For Your High Ticket Podcast Sales System Machine

By the time I am writing this book, I have interviewed 45 awesome six and seven-figure CEOs, Coaches, Service Business Owners, and Course Creators.

The first thing I do after publishing this book is reaching out to everyone I have interviewed on my podcast, asking them if they are interested in gifting my book to their current and prospective clients as a complimentary gift in their name.

Most of the guests you have interviewed on your podcast won't have any reservations about you sending their friends or contacts in their network who might need your book as a gift to them on their behalf.

Doing this will make something happen.

This will make them feel and look good in the eyes of their current and prospective clients and even people on their contact and email list.

With this, you are sending your books into the hand of the people who know the people you know as a result of your podcast.

Isn't this a great referrals machine?

I bet it is.

Or what better way is there to have people help you sell your service and brand to their friends and contacts without them feeling bad for doing that than this?

That's one way to use a Six Figure Business Book with your podcast to give more power to your High Ticket Podcast Sales System.

For every guest that comes to be interviewed on your podcast, you can also ask them to gift your book to their contacts after launching your book.

This will help you keep getting your books out in the hand of people who need to read them.

This is just the tip of the iceberg in combining your podcast and a Six Figure Business Book to get more sales for your business.

UP NEXT...

I've shown you how you can turn your podcast into a sales machine using The High Ticket Podcast Sales System.

In the two previous chapters, I have also shown you how you can combine the leverage your Six Figure Podcast offers with a Six Figure Business Book.

I love to show you the practicality of how I have used The High Ticket Podcast System to bring in revenue for one of my businesses.

Seeing is believing.

With all the things you have learned so far in this book, I love to show you one way all I have talked about worked for me.

Are you ready for some real-life examples of what The High Ticket Podcast Sales System can do?

If you are, flip to the next chapter, and let me show you that.

CHAPTER 6:
HOW I MADE $7500 IN JUST THREE WEEKS OF STARTING WITH JUST 13 EPISODES AND LESS THAN 500 DOWNLOADS FROM MY PODCAST

If you have made it this far, I must say well done.

This is where you will get the real gist of how I made $7600 from a podcast with only 13 episodes and less than five hundred downloads in just three weeks of starting my podcast.

Most podcasts, even the ones that were started years ago, never make this much, and most podcasts out there won't even make up to this.

This chapter is meant to brag to you.

If I want to brag, I have that bragging right, and I have earned that.

I include this chapter to show you the practicality of what you have learned so far in this book.

To show you how everything I have talked about in this book worked out for me in real life.

This result and all other ones I have got from implementing The High Ticket Podcast Sales System were a result of the intentionality I had when I started my fourth podcast.

After I had made those mistakes with my three previous podcasts, I knew I had to do something different from what I had done before.

I must tell you that my podcast has evolved a lot since I started.

I have refined my offer, changed my target audience, and changed my interview format.

These changes are made because of the feedback I got from implementing The High Ticket Podcast Sales System from its infancy stage to the stage where I have perfected the system much better.

My results now are better refined and better, and this is because I have cut out a lot of leakages in the system and the way I implemented it then.

I mentioned all of these to make you understand that the result you will read in this chapter happened when I hadn't refined The High Ticket Podcast Sales System as I have it now.

I created a video showing you how I made $7500 within the first 3 weeks of starting a podcast. You can watch the full video at TheSixFigurePodcast.com/Start to see how I did that and how you can do the same.

And now the full gist.

To start with, these are how I structured the podcast.

One of my two primary goals for my podcast is to have conversations with my ideal clients for my publishing company.

I built this in with the questions I asked my guests.

Those question naturally brings about a conversation about the idea or possibilities of my guest writing and publishing a book.

That same question also helps me to know if the person I am talking to needs my service or not, and also it helps me to know if I need to have a conversation about what I do with each guest.

Before or after my interview with my guest, I take some time to get to know them and ask questions about what they do and where they are now.

Most of my guests aren't a good fit for my service or need my help, but even for those people, It's always a win for me because I get to know them.

I have time to nurture my relationship with them, which has increased my network more than what I started with for all my years as an entrepreneur.

From my first thirty interviews, three of my guest became my guest, and the lifetime value of each client is $25k.

This doesn't include referrals I got from my satisfied clients. That is even more profitable than what came in for me directly from my podcast.

A bulk of your guests won't end up becoming a paying clients.

Most of my guests will not even hear about what I do or have me talk about what I do, and that's fine.

But with all my guests, I make sure I have an amazing time with them, and they also have a great time at the other end.

It's simply a win-win for us.

Also, remember, I am giving my guests a platform to share their stories, a platform to sell themselves and tell more people about what they do and who they are.

And also, the ultimate bonus for me from all my interviews is the relationships I can build with my guest.

I must say, my network is not what it used to be.

I now have more people I can network and connect with on a more personal and business level than before.

That, to me, is a big win for my podcast, a kind of secondary goal I had when I started the podcast.

Here it is to give you the brief gist of how I landed one of the guests as a client.

One of the questions I ask my guests is, "if you are to write a book now, what book will that be?"

This question is a harmless one that helped me determine if I should have a conversation with my guest about what I do then.

On asking that question, Victor told me he is in the process of writing one, but he is stuck in the process and doesn't know what to do.

After the interview, I asked him if we could have another call to help me understand where he is in the process of writing his book and how I could be of help.

Mind you, I wasn't selling anything to him but offering to see how I can help him move forward, at least from where he is in the process.

He said yes, and he scheduled a call with me, we had that call, and I listened to him tell me where he was.

From there, I told him how he could move forward, and since I have a service that could help him become a published author from where he is now, I told him how I could help him and what I could do for him with my service.

He said yes, and we had a contract, and payment followed.

Note that, right from the beginning of the sales process that started from my question during the interview, I didn't come as a salesman who wanted to sell him on him becoming my client.

One conversation led to another, and we both realized we could work together to make his dream a reality.

This is how my conversations have turned into business relationships using this system.

I want to remind you that many people I've had as a guest don't fit well into whom I can help.

This is one area I have improved on since I started m podcast.

I now have my ideal client figured out: those are the people I invite or accept invitations from to be a guest on my podcast.

I also need to let you know that not everyone who is an ideal client who becomes your guest will become a paying client.

I have since modified my offer to focus on helping people replicate my result using The High Ticket Podcast Sales System to tap into the power of a Six Figure Podcast and a Six Figure Business Book.

This change of direction has helped me narrow down whom I can serve.

For those I now serve, I got more results for them than I used to get when my focus was only on helping my people to write and publish a book.

I want you not to have any expectation of landing everyone who said yes to be your guest as a client.

Even with the right people coming as guests, many won't be ready to do business, and only a few will be in that buying mood.

You can follow up over time with everyone you interview who is not ready, which is also what The High Ticket Podcast Sales System can do for you.

I talked about how to use this system to create a never-ending referral on demand for your business.

You can pick up a copy of my book - The High Ticket Podcast Sales System, to learn more about that.

You can see how the sales process for my business started naturally from my conversations with my guests.

With this system, I am winning in more ways than money.

And I love that this podcasting system meets all my criteria for what I have been looking for since 2020.

It's scalable.

To get more clients, you need to talk to more guests, and at a point, you can remove yourself from the process by having another host.

It's measurable.

I love data and feedback. I don't think you should blame me for this.

With a diploma and bachelor's degree in Computer Science, I've formed the habit of thinking and talking in numbers.

You should know the average lifetime value of each client you land on from your podcast. With this, you should be able to afford to spend money to produce as many episodes as you can in a month.

You can also figure out what type of guests you should have on your podcast to close more if you want.

All the data you need to make this system work well can be measured.

It's also a system you own and control.

Unlike ads, your posts on social media, and even your videos on YouTube, you own all your interview files.

You own and control all your guests' contact and almost everything you need for this system to work.

If one podcast host messes up, it takes just a click to migrate all your past episodes to another host.

I just love the fact that you have all processes and systems you have in all of those under your control and authority.

Goodbye to the day when you will make a lot of money from Facebook or Google ads, and the next day, it will stop working, or you will wake up to see your account has been banned.

It's also repeatable.

I love my time interviewing my guests and listening to them share a lot about themselves and their businesses.

You will also love it as you learn the rope.

You can repeat that as long as you want, and if tomorrow the podcast grows more than you can handle, you can hire someone to be the host.

And ultimately, this system is duplicable.

You would have processes to help you churn out as many episodes as possible.

I have virtual assistants who work with me to produce the show.

I edited the first ten episodes myself, but I have hired two assistants who do that for me.

All I just do now is interview my guests and play with my wife.

I also have a process that books guests for me.

All of these can be replicated and duplicated.

With all I have learned from The Six Figure Entrepreneur Podcast, I can start another podcast, replicate this same system, and get results.

I am doing that with past guests, and I love the results.

You also can replicate this system to start another podcast if you want to.

Now tell me, what form of client accusation system offers all these?

UP NEXT...

This whole book turned the table on what you have learned about podcasting.

To succeed with podcasts, especially if your motive for podcasting is to make money and use it to sell more of your services, you need to have a mindset shift from the norms.

In the next chapter, I have some tips I love to give you, and I will also show you how you can replicate The High Ticket Podcast Sales System for your business to get the result you want in terms of more high ticket clients.

CHAPTER 7: MY UNCONVENTIONAL ADVICE ABOUT PODCASTING AND HOW TO REPLICATE THE HIGH PODCAST SALES SYSTEM FOR YOUR BUSINESS

Being a guru is one thing I don't ever want to become. I don't want to sound like or act like one podcast guru.

I am just a guy who found something he has been looking for.

I also want you to read this book and put everything you have learned in this book to the test.

But I know one thing.

I have started three podcasts in the past, and I failed them.

And with my fourth, I stuck gold without having any of the bell and whistle associated with having a podcast.

I am just talking about what worked for me, and if you like, you can try it and see if it works.

And I must say, if you love to try this and love me to guide you, you can jump on a call with me here to discuss that.

PLANNING TO START A PODCAST? THESE ARE WHAT YOU SHOULD KNOW

If you care to listen to my unconventional advice and if you are planning to start a podcast, then here we go.

1. Have A Plan

By having a plan, I don't mean you should have the same plan that podcast gurus have taught you.

The only time you should listen to those common things podcast gurus are saying is if you have a large audience, you can launch your podcast to get lots of downloads.

What I mean by a plan is knowing what you want and seeing how starting a podcast can help you get that, and if you don't see a podcast helping you achieve your goals, then you should do something else.

2. If You Want To Start A Podcast To Sell Your Services Or Products To An Audience Or Even Make Money From Sponsorships And You Don't Have An Audience, And A Big One At That, Don't Waste Your Time Podcasting.

Build an audience first, and start a podcast when you have one.

There is some exception to this anyway, and they are:

- Podcasting can work for you in this case if you have a lot of money to spend on ads and podcast sponsorship on big podcasts.
- If you just want to have fun podcasting without any expectations in terms of monetary or other forms of gains.

3. If You Don't Have An Audience And You Have Business With A High Ticket Offer To Sell, Then Podcasting This Way I Have Talked About In This Book, Is One Thing You Should Try Your Hand At.

Your best bet to get clients is to start a podcast for your ideal clients.

This will help you to have conversations with your ideal clients, and maybe if you do a good job with those conversations, you can get some to become your clients.

As mentioned in this book, note that this system won't work for you if you don't have a high ticket offer, services, or products to sell.

This isn't a system you can use to sell your $99 or $399 course, ebook, or masterclass.

It won't be worth your time having a podcast using this system if you don't have a service that commands a high price point to make it worth the hassles and work it takes to set up, run and manage this system.

I can afford to spend between $1500 and $2000 a month producing my podcast, knowing closing one client in a month is enough to keep paying such money and more for my podcast while still having enough to take home as profit.

Will you spend $1500 or more a month to produce a podcast only to sell two or three $299 courses?

That isn't good math to build a six or seven-figure business on.

3. Unless you love the idea of having the bragging right of saying you have a podcast that gets tons of thousands of downloads, metrics like the number of downloads, the number of the subscriber, social media followers, and email list size are vanity metrics you should pay little or no attention to.

I don't give a damn about all of these. You should care less about them as well.

The number of relationships I built over time and the balance in my stripe account are the only metrics I pay attention to.

If you are unknown or just starting, maybe you should do yourself some good, shut your ears to all that the Podcast gurus are saying and pay no attention to all of those.

Don't get me wrong here.

I am not saying having an audience or building one isn't important.

I surely have a budget for building one, but my point is this.

A podcast for people who don't have an existing audience is not the right or good way to build an audience.

If I need to build an email list, I would rather spend money on kinds of stuff like Facebook ads, creating Youtube videos, or blogging to build a list, and even with those, nothing is guaranteed.

UP NEXT...

CHAPTER 8:
ISSUES YOU MIGHT RUN INTO AND MISTAKES YOU NEED TO AVOID WITH YOUR SIX FIGURE PODCAST

ISSUES YOU MIGHT ENCOUNTER WITH YOUR SIX FIGURE PODCAST

I won't tell you how awesome having a Six Figure Podcast has been for me since I started implementing all you have learned in this book without telling you about the challenges I faced implementing this unique podcast system.

Having gone through various versions of this system, there are two issues I have encountered and ones you might run into as well.

And to cap it all, there are some mistakes I will talk about that you need to avoid with your Six Figure Podcast if you are to get the right result implementing The High Ticket Podcast Sales System

1. Guests Not Showing Up

I had some people I reached out to who booked a time for an interview with me who ended up not showing up.

When I looked at what might be the cause of that, I realized it was an issue with my follow-up with anyone who has booked a time to be a guest on my show.

I overcame that by switching from Calendly to ScheduleOnce, which has a feature that allows me to send more reminders to my guest before our scheduled time.

Now, I send a reminder a day before our interview, another one an hour before, and another fifteen minutes before the interview.

Since then, I haven't had anyone not show up.

You need to use a scheduling tool with a multiple follow-ups feature.

Not having one in place can be a costly mistake that will result in guests not showing up for your interview with them.

2. Not Knowing Who Your Ideal Clients Are

I started with the idea that my target clients are coaches and consultants because those are the people I have worked with in the past, but after having conversations with fifteen people who fit well into what I think is my ideal clients, I realized my best fit is busy CEOs.

I discovered this due to the data I gathered from my first 20 interviews.

The people who need me and what I have to offer most are my guests, who are CEOs and Founders.

My first and second high-paying clients from my podcasts are all busy CEOs.

And, as I said before, my emotions can lie, but data won't lie.

And at a point down the line, I discovered I like to work by changing my offer based on where I am and the results I want for my clients.

Right now, my ideal clients are different.

Not having a clear glimpse of who your ideal client are and what type of result you want to get for them can be a painful mistake you will want to avoid.

The good news is that despite a lot of wasted time, I had brought many people who weren't a good fit for my business to be my guests in the initial time of starting my podcast.

I used that feedback to learn who I wanted to work with and whom I should bring to be guests on my podcasts.

If you already have a business that has all these figured out, your result will come faster and be much better than what I got when I started my podcast.

5 MISTAKES YOU NEED TO AVOID WITH YOUR SIX FIGURE PODCAST

The High Ticket Podcast Sales System, when implemented the right way, will fill your high ticket service sale pipeline with clients.

But care must be taken to ensure you avoid mistakes that could ruin your chance of making The High Ticket Podcast Sales System work for you.

One thing you must take note of is the fact that this system is based on podcasting.

If you look around, people make a lot of mistakes when they start a podcast, but since you are reading this book right now, these are the mistakes you should avoid to ensure you get the best results from implementing The High Ticket Podcast Sales System.

1. Going For A-List And Popular Names As Your Guest.

The conventional podcasting plan is to interview the Seth Godin or Gary Vaynerchuk of this world on your podcast.

Many podcasters aim for this with the hope these A-list guests will share their podcast with their audience, which will make them famous and help them build a big audience from the traffic they will get from such interviews.

Please don't do that.

You should aim to land A-list guests on your podcast only if those A-list guests are your target audience.

If A-list guests aren't ideal clients, you should ignore them when looking for people to interview for your Six Figure Podcasts.

Most times, your ideal clients would be people who aren't famous or well-known in their space, and that's fine.

This is an advantage for you and your podcast because those people don't get much exposure like the A-listers, and many might have never been invited before to be a guest on any podcast.

This is why you will likely get a yes when you invite them to be your guest.

For the Gary Vee, Tim Ferris, and co of this world, they get too many invites to be a guest on podcasts, summits, and conferences.

What's your chance of getting a yes from these people to appear as a guest on your relatively unknown or new podcast?

2. Not Knowing Who Your Ideal Clients Are

This one is a very big mistake you should avoid.

To make The High Ticket Podcast Sales System work well for you, you must be clear about who your ideal clients are.

And forget about the popular ideal client's avatar you might have encountered online when looking for a way to nail down your ideal clients.

You don't need to make things difficult for yourself.

Just ask yourself what you sell, the solution you provide, and what problem your solution solves; these will help you nail down whom you can help with your service.

You might not have it all figured out at the start, and that's fine, but the beauty of using The High Ticket Podcast Sales System is that you have the framework to change a lot over time when you get feedback from all you have done.

When I started The Six Figure Entrepreneur Podcast, I was clear about what I have to offer, but due to the nature of what I offer, I have more than one type of people I can help. As time pass by, I keep understanding who is the best among these many archetypes of people I can help who need me most and the ones I can help the most.

If, like me, you have more than one type of person you can help with your high ticket service, pick one of them, get started, and wait for some time to get feedback.

If things aren't working with those targets, you can change things, which is easy to do with this system.

3. Focusing On What Doesn't Matter

It's easy to pay attention to kinds of stuff like the number of downloads your podcast has, the number of people subscribing to your podcast on iTunes, the best microphone to use, and many mundane things.

Those things and many more aren't important or even worth thinking about.

The only things you want to focus on are:

- Your ideal clients, referrals partners, and partners you want to invite to your podcast will be your guest.

- A medium to reach out to them, like LinkedIn, Cold emailing, etc., and another medium to schedule an interview that removes any back-and-forth messaging for scheduling.
- A podcast that gives you the platform to interview your ideal clients.
- Get on a call with your guests and interview them. There are a lot of platforms that will help you do that and for a start and the simplest way for you, use Zoom.
- A production system that will edit, produce and publish your podcast. For best results, you should outsource this part as you have no reason to worry about all the technicalities of producing a podcast.

To make life easy for you, visit www.thesixfigureentrepreneur.com/podcast-production-call to book a call with me here to hook you up with my podcast production team that can help you take care of all this technical stuff while you show up to interview your guests and have time to run your business.

Anything that isn't on this list is just a distraction and waste of time that doesn't deserve your attention.

4. Seeing And Implementing The High Ticket Podcast Sales System From The Saleman Point Of View

If well implemented, everything you read in this book has the power to transform your business and give you tremendous results.

With a powerful sales system like this comes the responsibility of ensuring you implement it with the best intent and from the right point of view.

Your Six Figure Podcast isn't about you, nor is any part or component of it about you.

It's about your ideal clients, people who will be your guest on your podcast.

Apart from the first episode, which is like a thriller for The Six Figure Entrepreneur Podcast in which I introduce anyone listening to the podcast to who I am and why I started the podcast, none of my podcast episodes is about me.

There aren't any episodes in which I talk about myself.

Your job with your Podcast using The High Ticket Podcast Sales System is to shine the spotlight onto your guests, the people you might likely work with later on.

You want to make them feel good about themselves, talk about themselves, and give them a platform (your Podcast) where they can showcase who they are, what they do, and more about themselves.

They are the hero of the whole show, not you.

So this isn't a platform where all you do is talk about yourself, what you do, and even what you offer or sell.

Also, your job using The High Ticket Podcast Sales System isn't that of a salesman.

Your job is that of a Spotlight(er), a Friend to your guests, and a Solution Provider if they need your help.

You are not to sell your guest while interviewing them or make your interview be a sale pitch where you try to get them to buy from you.

If you do this, you won't get any results with the system; your guest will not like you or want to talk to you again, and you will waste your time and resources to produce your podcast.

This is because, despite your ideal clients needing you and your service, they won't like you to invite them for what is to be something about them and now see you make it all about you and your business.

Turning your guests into clients will happen naturally when you get to know them, what they do, and what they need help with.

Your pre-interview and post-interview conversations should take care of these.

When done well, the sales conversations will just be natural results of building rapport and trust with your guests while they now see you as a friend who can help with their problems.

This is how I have turned some of my guests into paid clients without selling them anything or talking about myself.

But a word of caution here.

You want to make sure your guests know what you do, and there is a subtle way of doing this, like you doing that in a simple intro before you start interviewing them.

5. Trying To Handle The Production Of Your Podcast By Yourself

Before I started The Six Figure Entrepreneur Podcast, I started three other podcasts in ten years, and with all of them, I am the podcast host, editor, show note writer, and podcast producer.

No wonder I quit all of them before my 20th episode.

When I started The Six Figure Entrepreneur Podcast, I did all of these things myself for the first ten episodes, and in the space of two weeks, I almost got sick from sitting for hours editing and producing my podcast episodes.

But I came to a point where I knew doing everything myself, even though I know how to do them, is the best way to burn out and quit before I can start getting results.

And again, when I remember why I started the podcast, which is to have a scalable, measurable, consistent, and efficient way to fill up my sales pipeline with paying clients, I knew doing everything myself wasn't capable and efficient.

And that's when I hired two assistants to help me deal with all the editing, production, and publishing stuff that would have to take my time.

From my 11th episode, I was able to move faster to interview more guests and have more conversations, and right now, I have added more people to my production team to cater to the needs of some of my clients who also need help with their podcast production.

Don't do all this stuff by yourself.

Doing so is a sure way to burn out and quit before you even have the right foundation to have a well-oiled High Ticket Podcast Sales System.

Get help to handle all of the backends, and the only good thing you can do is to show up and interview your guests.

Even when you might want to scale, you can outsource the interview part and just focus on working with your client and running your business.

Get in touch with me at www.thesixfigureentrepreneur.com/podcast-production-call and let's have a chat to hook you up with my production team to help you handle all the technical stuff that goes with your High Ticket Podcast Sales System.

6. Not Having A Well Refined Offer To Sell

I struggled a lot with this at the initial stage of my podcast.

I didn't have a clear offer, and I wasted a lot of time and had some opportunities to close some deals that went away because I didn't have a picture of the right thing I was offering.

When you have guests who are your ideal clients, you need a well-defined and valuable offer to give those who want to know more about what you do.

This will make life easier for you than just jumping on calls with your guests without any tangible offer at hand for those who want to do business with you.

Before you start your Six Figure Podcast, my advice is for you to get clarity on two things:

- Who are your ideal clients.
- What you are selling to them.

Having these two things figured out will help you get a better and faster result from all your effort, time, and money you will put on the line to create and produce your Six Figure Podcast.

UP NEXT...

I always like to include a question-and-answer chapter in all my books to make sure I answer common questions I have been asked before and ones my readers might want to ask me.

This book won't be an exception

In the next chapter, I will answer some questions I have seen my clients ask me before and ones I feel you might have after reading this book.

CHAPTER 9: FREQUENTLY ASKED QUESTIONS

In this chapter, I will answer those questions and some that I believe you might want to ask me after reading this book.

QUESTION #1: WILL THIS SYSTEM WORK LIKE YOU SAID

If you need to hear it again, I will say it again.

This works and does so incredibly well without you running ads, building a list, doing webinars, or posting on social media 24/7.

The only caveat here is that it works well for selling high-ticket offers.

The results of implementing this system go beyond getting clients.

It also offers you the most efficient way to connect, network, and build relationships with your ideal clients and decision-makers space.

QUESTION #2:
WHY WILL ANYONE WANT TO BE A GUEST ON MY PODCAST WHEN I AM JUST STARTING AND HAVE NO AUDIENCE

Good question.

The reason why your ideal clients will want to be guests on your show is this:

- Unless your ideal clients are popular people, celebrities, or top-in-demand influencers, being asked to be a featured guest on podcasts or even any other form of media is a rare event, making it a valuable ask for them to get a yes.
- Everyone likes having a spotlight shining on them.

  We all want to feel appreciated, important, and recognized, and if you remember, one of your primary goals for your Podcast is to shine the spotlight on your guest, share their stories or expertise and open them up to a world that doesn't know they exist.

  Who will say no to that anyway?

- Your ideal clients want to tell their stories or share their expertise with the world, but they might be too busy or clueless about how to get that done. Your podcast is an opportunity for them to do that without any cost in whatever way to them.

They only need to show, and they know you are doing the dirty job of taking all they say during the interview with you and turning it into a machine that helps them achieve their goal.

- I've cold-emailed a lot of six and seven figures entrepreneurs, busy business executives, CEOs, and Founders of successful startups to be guests on The Six-Figure Entrepreneur Podcast, and I have got many requests for guest appearances as well.

So far, I've only got a few people saying no to me, and of interest is the fact that the few people who said no gave reasons that have nothing to do with me or my podcast but about their inability to jump on a call with me die to personal or business reason.

Data and numbers don't lie.

So if you need assurance, you can take that from real-life data I have gathered in my quest to implement and perfect this system.

QUESTION #3: WHAT DO I SAY TO MAKE PEOPLE BE A GUEST ON MY PODCAST

This is simple.

Just ask!

My first emails were sent to guests that appeared on a popular entrepreneurship podcast I've followed for years.

I was so nervous as to what I will write in those emails.

I spent days researching the best cold email to send that will get me a yes.

But one thing keeps coming to my mind, which is this.

In 2015, after publishing the first installment of my Memoir, Life Hacking, I wanted to get some eyeballs and ride on the shoulders of some influencers to launch the book.

I emailed two popular self-help bloggers and then asked them to write a forward for my book.

I got a yes, which is how my book has two forewords from two popular self-help influencers.

I asked guys like John Less Dumas, Neil Patel, John Corcoran, Derek Sivers, and 30 other top internet celebrities to contribute to a round-up post I planned to launch my new blog and book.

The post was a success, even though I am kind of clueless about what to do with the traffic and spotlight I got then.

All these happened from asking these busy influencers what I wanted, and that was it.

You don't need to think much about what to write or say to get your ideal clients to be a guest on your podcast.

Just ask!

That's what I did after spending days trying to find cold email templates I could use.

The best template I have seen to work well is me just introducing myself and telling them why I want them to be guests on my podcast and asking them if they are in.

That's it.

QUESTION #4: WHAT'S THE BEST MIC YOU RECOMMEND I USE

This also is another thing you should not worry about.

For starters, visit www.thesixfigureentrepreneur.com/headset-micget this headset with a microphone.

It's the most basic mic you can use for your podcast, and it works fine
How do I know that?

That was the headset I used for my first ten episodes before buying a more expensive one.

For recommendations, here are three great microphones you can buy.

Visit www.thesixfigureentrepreneur.com/Blue-Snowball-Mic to get the Blue Snowball Mic.

Visit www.thesixfigureentrepreneur.com/Blue-Yeti-Mic to get the Blue Yeti Microphone.

Visit www.thesixfigureentrepreneur.com/ATR-2005-Mic to get the ATR-2005 Microphone.

The mic you use isn't one of the things you should worry about.

That is just one of the many 80% things that only add 20% results to your baseline.

And if you want to have your podcast system done for you without having to worry about all of the technical stuff, visit www.thesixfigureentrepreneur.com/podcast-production-call to **book a call with me** and let's have a discussion to get you started.

QUESTION #5: WHAT DO I CALL MY PODCAST

Good question.

The answer to this is also simple.

Give a name to your podcast that ticks all these boxes:

- Speaks to your ideal clients who are also your podcast guest.

  My guests and ideal clients are six and seven-figure entrepreneurs, and it's an easy decision to call my podcast The Six Figure Entrepreneur Podcast since those are my guests. Also, my podcast is meant to share their stories.

- It should not be about what your business does or your expertise but something that your ideal clients and guest will be able to connect with.

Make your podcast and your podcast name be about what your guests/ideal clients care about or have something to share about.

QUESTION #6:
ISN'T THIS SYSTEM A DECEITFUL WAY TO DO BUSINESS

I was on a call with Matt Hansen, CEO of Hansen Holdings, a super busy guy who has built a multi-million dollar real estate investment business.

During our conversation, he mentioned he wanted to write a book and had started one but abandoned it because he didn't have the time to finish it.

I can help him; this is what my team and I have been doing for years.

During our post-interview chat, he asked me to tell him about myself, my business, and how I could help him get his book back to life.

I didn't ask him to do that, but he knew I had a book publishing company that could help him (from my podcast intro), he had a need I could help with, and he asked me how I couldn't help him.

Do you think I deceived him into doing business with him?

Of course not.

My interview with Matt was amazing; he enjoyed his time with me, and I enjoyed my time with him and learned some useful tips about real estate investment.

Asking him to be a guest on my podcast was a win-win for him, me, and anyone who listens to the podcast episode.

That is a big win, and the business part is a bonus.

And Matt and all of my guests, who are smart and successful business executives, would have called me off my bullshit if they thought I deceived them into doing business with me by inviting them to be featured on my podcast.

I am adding value to them, and they know that smartly.

I am also smart to know that 80% of my guests won't become my client or will even need what I have to offer or be in the right position to hire me. For all these amazing entrepreneurs, nothing like a business conversation happens between us.

It's just purely me helping them to share their stories.

For the 20% who fit well into whom I can work with, they are happy they got to know me because I became a solution to a piece of news they have, and as a business-minded guy, I will take that and feel good about it.

You aren't doing anything deceitful here.

You are adding value to your guests, and if everything else aligns, you get to help them solve a problem they have with your high-ticket offer.

But don't be a jerk by making your podcast or interviews be about you and not about them.

That, to me, is the greatest sin and the purest form of deceit you can imagine.

Make it all about them, have fun and friendly conversations with your guests, and become their friends, and your friends who need you or want to do business with you will let you know that.

For the rest of your friends who won't become your client, you have just added to your network and net worth, a relationship you can nurture over time.

QUESTION #7: I DON'T LIKE MY VOICE. DO YOU THINK I SHOULD START A PODCAST?

I don't like my voice, nor do I like to have my face on camera.

But I show up, and none of my guests have complained about my voice or even my accent (newsflash, I wasn't born a native English speaker and I have a slight non-English accent, but I know what I am doing, know my stuff in and out and have a lot to offer my guests).

Instead, most of my guests listened to my past episodes and said they enjoyed what they listened to during my interview.

My emotions can tell me I have a bad voice, but the number and data from my guests don't agree with my emotions, and just to tell you this, I am the guy who likes to follow data over emotions.

Nobody cares or will care about your voice, but they care so much about how you make them feel and what you offer.

I don't do videos when interviewing my guests, even though some of them will open their cameras for me to see them.

I am just not comfortable showing my face, which might not change in the near future, but I make my guests' time with me memorable. I asked them questions that made them want to talk about their entrepreneurial journey and the stories and lessons they had picked along the way.

They will remember all that and not how thick of an accent I have.

And if you are an American or native English speaker reading this, you have no excuse not to get your butt out there and start a podcast using my simple implement High Ticket Podcast Sales System that you have been reading about in this book.

Your face looks don't matter, and if you think you have a lovely camera-friendly face, turn on your camera, and if you don't feel good about showing your face, turn off your camera and shine with whatever voice you have.

QUESTION #8: CAN THIS WORK FOR NEW BUSINESS I JUST STARTED?

Absolutely yes.

I've used this system to start two new businesses from scratch to profitability in less than a month.

And these are businesses that sell high-end, high-ticket offers.

You don't need any prior clout, you don't need an audience, and neither do you need to be known in your space.

Your podcast, if done right, is the best way to get all of these over time. And that's is of you care about all of that.

QUESTION #9:
I HAVE OTHER QUESTIONS. HOW CAN I REACH YOU?

Sure.

I love to hear from you.

Just shoot me an email at Hello@TheSixFigureEntrepreneur.com.

I send a lot of emails every day. That's what my business feeds on.

And I love to receive emails in my inbox.

Just ask, remember?

UP NEXT...

You have learned a lot from this book, no doubt.

I will like to end this book on a note that shows you what to do after reading this book to get started to have your Six Figure Podcast, and if you already have a podcast, how you can take things further to make that shift to embracing the Six Figure Podcast ideology.

CHAPTER 10:
HOW CAN YOU GET STARTED WITH YOUR SIX FIGURE PODCAST

It doesn't take much to get started.

You need:

- A high ticket service you can sell.
- Have an idea of who your ideal clients are. Don't worry if you don't have this figured out like me.

  You can start with whom you have in mind and then collect the data to know who fits well into the picture of your ideal clients.

- A podcast that can help you have conversations with your ideal clients.
- A good mic. You can get one on Amazon for $100 or more.
- A Calendly account for a start
- A podcast host. There are tons of free podcast hosts, and if you don't have money to throw at this, an option like Anchor will work best for you
- A Zoom account

If you have all of these, you are ready to get started.

I must say replicating this system requires you to deal with the technical parts like equipment, hosting, getting guests, etc.

You also need to deal with the strategy part, like what questions you are to ask your guests to make them have a good conversation with you and vice versa, and how and when you can bring up conversations about what you do and how your guests can work with you.

For the technical parts, my seven-year-old niece (by the time this book goes to press anyway) can start a podcast talking about her love for color painting, but for the strategy parts, you can mess things up if you don't know what to do or how to do them.

At the core of your High Ticket, Podcast Sales Systems is your Six Figure Podcast and The Six Figure Business Book.

When you combine two of those, you have one badass of a system that will continually flood your business with qualified and easy-to-sell clients for your high-ticket service offers.

And from what I have seen so far implementing all I showed you in this book, it's also funding to all of this.

At the time of writing this chapter, I had just finished an interview with an amazing six-figure entrepreneur, and it was a blast from the beginning to the end.

This is one human I would never get to know or talk to if not for my podcast.

Beyond the benefits of using this system, the sheer fun I am having interviewing my guest and helping those who like to work with me from the basis of being friends rather than me being a salesman is enough for me to keep doing all of these you have learned in this book.

With your Six Figure Podcast and your Six Figure Business Book, selling won't even feel like what selling used to be for you, and on top of that, you will be building tons of relationships, making many new friends, and building up your network over time.

But all of these won't happen when you do nothing.

You now have a system that can bring in more clients for your business without doing all those sales-y kinds of stuff many business owners as you do.

And you also now have a system that will bring in referrals for your business from current clients, past clients, prospective clients, and even guests you will interview on your podcast to add value to them and make it easy for them to refer clients to you.

And you also have a system you can tap in to never let any client slip through your hands if they are not in the "ready to buy" phase. That is a follow-up system you can use to stay on top of the minds of your past guests and prospective clients who are not ready to buy from you.

This is the power you will have when implementing The High Ticket Podcast Sales System.

I look forward to hearing the good news about your success in implementing The High Ticket Podcast Sales System.

And I hope this book has opened your eyes to a whole new way of thinking and a new reality of how to be a human when you need to sell to another human.

To take things to the next level for you, I want you to win, to implement everything you have learned in this book.

When you are ready, here are ways my team and I at The Six Figure Entrepreneur can help you:

1. Be My Special Guest On The Six Figure Podcast Show

This exclusive offer is available to only those who pick up a copy of this book and read it, and it's not the typical guest I host on The Six Figure Podcast Show.

This is just for you – because you pick a copy of my book or one given to you by someone who knows me or has been in touch with me.

We will jump on a call and brainstorm how you can implement The High Ticket Podcast Sales System for your business.

My team will have that call recorded, edited, and published as an episode of The Six Figure Podcast Show.

On this podcast, I usually interview entrepreneurs with a podcast and have something to sell to share how they are using their podcasts to bring in more revenue for their businesses and how they are making money from their podcast. Visit https://www.TheSixFigureePodcast.com/Feature and let's have some fun.

2. Get Help In Setting Up Your Six Figure Podcast

There is a lot to deal with when starting a podcast as a beginner.

If you love to create and start your Six Figure Podcast using what you have learned in this book, and you want to have all the processes taken care of by my team at The Six Figure Entrepreneur.

Visit https://www.TheSixFigurePodcast.com/Start Book a call with me here, and let's chat about how you can get started immediately.

3. Need Help Writing, Publishing And Launching Your Six Figure Business Book Without Writing A Word

My life changed the day I wrote my first Six Figure Business Book.

If the idea of having your Six Figure Business Book to enjoy all the benefits that come with it, which you have learned in this book, visit https://www.TheBookCot.com/Consult to apply and book a call to have become The Book Cot's latest Six Figure Business Book author.

My team has the expertise, strategies, and processes to take you from just a book idea to having your Six Figure Buisness Book in your hands in three months or less.

4. Get On A Call With Me

If you are interested in working with me to set up your High Ticket Podcast Sales System after reading this book, visit https://www.TheSixFigurePodcast.com/Start to book a 40 minutes strategy call with me.

On this strategy call, I will sit down with you to look at your business and how The High Ticket Podcast Sales System can help you land more high ticket clients, get more referrals and expand your network.

We can then talk about how to implement the High Ticket Podcast.

ABOUT THE AUTHOR

Mayowa Ajisafe is an author, book coach, and founder of **The Six Figure Entrepreneur**, a business growth agency that helps high ticket service business owners to attract more clients and 10x their revenue.

He is also the host of **The Six Figure Entrepreneur Podcast** and **The Six Figure Podcast Show**.

He is also the founder of The Book Cot, a publishing agency that helps busy high-end entrepreneurs write, publish and launch their Six Figure Business Books.

He loves to sit in his virtual space and interview outstanding entrepreneurs who have built a six-seven and eight-figure businesses from scratch to share their entrepreneurial journey with the world.

For more information about **The Six Figure Entrepreneur Program**, **The High Ticket Podcast Sales System**, and **The Six Figure Business Book**, visit https://www.TheSixFigureEntrepreneur.com and https://www.TheSixFigurePodcast.com or send an email to Hello@TheSixFigureEntrepreneur.com.

For more information about The Book Cot's six steps to writing, publishing, and launching a Six Figure Business Book in three months or less, visit https://www.TheBookCot.com

www.ingramcontent.com/pod-product-compliance
Lightning Source LLC
Chambersburg PA
CBHW041640050326
40690CB00027B/5283